180 Pounds of Poet Meat

by Garri Saganenko

Jim,   June 8, 2023

Thank you for supporting my work.
I hope you find something in
here that is meaningful to you.
Also, I never learned how to
write my last name in cursive.

— Jim Saganenko

Garri ☺

2020-23
COVER CONCEPT: GARRI SAGANENKO
COVER CONCEPT AND DESIGN: ABIGAIL MAKER
INTERIOR LAYOUT: KEN BAUMANN
ISBN: 978-0-578-39918-8
© *2023 Garri Saganenko*
1st Edition, 1st Printing
June 2023
Printed by Spencer Printing in Honesdale, PA

CERTIFIED FREE
OR THE SEA
THE OCEAN
OF
REFERENCE TO

Table of Contents

Note to the Reader

This book is best when read aloud
by the author with nobody around.

It is next best when read aloud
by the author to strangers who
listen and make strange sounds.

Wittgenstein: You know, I'd quite like to have composed a philosophical work that consisted entirely of jokes.

Keynes: Why didn't you?

— *Wittgenstein* (1993)

Light Meat

(Lighter, Leaner)

I Dream of *Poet Meat*

180 Pounds of Poet Meat appeared
in my dream last night.

Finally, it had been published,
placed on a shelf at the bookstore
on the campus of St. John's College
in Santa Fe.

A lone male.
A kind and nourishing mother.
And I a nourished son.

I pulled the book from the shelf,
walked over to the checkout counter
and showed the clerk what I had done.

The brilliant cover, the bare spine,
the skillful binding — they could
not *believe* it had been self-published,
that I had paid my own money to
make a book without feeling
embarrassed or ashamed
that it, too, lacked the seal
of Knopf or Penguin or any
of those other fancy names.

"But it looks so *good*."

I swooned, until we pushed
aside the matte white cover
and discovered a transparent pink
film had been pasted across each
page of poems plus photographs too.

A transparent pink page smeared (!)
with McDonald's chicken nugget goo.

What a terrifying look.

In effect, the film functioned
as rose-colored glasses
for the entire book.

We stared awhile —
confused, flushed, demure.

Then the dream shut up and out shot:

"Humming dandelion
makes bluish lips go 'Brrrrr!'"

A Short Poem On Toast
Written for an Old Friend
About Whose Artwork
I Often Boast

Friend,

Believe you me I am finally
beginning to see why I shouldn't
use the same spreader for peanut
butter as I do for jam and jelly.

And, what is better,

we   just   may   be

finally

in possession of the same taste,

the same.....sen-si-bility.

The Art Milk Life (At Seventeen)

Quickly ubiquitized - I rushed red hot
on flat tires in order not to draw the ire
of those who might paddle my adolescence
into submission for time is the teacher
to the boy who learns a series of several lessons.

At how-to-be I was guessing.

I sold myself to the grocery store and then hid
in the trash to read *The Fountainhead*.

I told you I flushed yellow, but I really flushed red.

As far as trash —

I myself am still stashed past
the yellow tags counter-clockwise
to the produce and as far as profitable
from the magical motion-sensing door.

Only 'wags call boys fags — it's terrible —
but in *Une Charogne* Baudelaire writes
"*Comme une femme lubrique*," which
roughly translates to "Like a whore."

And at seventeen milk made art everything
and made of me only simple demands;
bottles had burst and sprayed all over
Scott Gurry's 30 rack of devil may cry cans.

I contemplated a life aligned to the legion
of this now clearly troubled man — but I came
into the cold whenever to suffer late the hours
because Scotty Gurry required with a pallett

of snotty dairy the help of my precious ejaculate
hands.

Some boys *do* dream to live by the coolers of cream.

And why not?

I could more easily pick out all the old perishables
than open my closet to find clothes that were wearable.

Others were doof nosed but Richie gave me Snus.
We retrieved carts, doted upon Plugra, and wondered
whether the United Food and Commercial Workers
served any actual use.

I argued Yes, it protects me from the likes
of Tammy, Judy, and Shirley.

These three ladies couldn't care less
that I signed up to play flute precisely
because it was considered to be girly.

Later, I swallowed Richie's tobacco
and wanted to puke.

It gave me salsa tummy, turned my art milk
life sour and became an emetic smelling
slightly of the faintest, strangest fruit.

This is my one life, I didn't choose.

Track practice was <u>long</u>.

The Union kept me from getting fired.

Out on the bench behind the carts
I slept to rid myself of being tired.

It was a strange time for milk
and the question was whether
to skip skim.

I drank chocolate *every day*
while squeaky emo girls dressed
in pajama bottoms with imagery
from the short-lived children's
show *Invader Zim*.

Then there was the Weatherman.

Puking in the bathroom.

A sign of circumspection.

Brautigan got his mayonnaise
and I finally got my erection.

Quick! Say something trite, like:
Sometimes all a young man needs
is a [knowing] push in the right direction.

My brother, he labeled me "Garelick"
because my ass had a milky white complexion.

I want to be the Belle
of Amherst – or at
least the ball.

I want to Piss Myself
from Bright's Disease
– and then take a fall.

I want to lie –that's true –
and then –a discovery! –
Some Pretty gosh
darn good Poetry....

The Gift My Dentist Gave Me

Hygienist asked, so I said:
"Bubblegum!"

Then they'd dip the bristles
into a penny spot of paste
and start the hum.

I did this every
six months for
nearly a decade.

Flavor all over my teeth —
those sneaky pockets
beneath the tongue
where mushy crackers
are known to clung.

Is my mouth a washing machine
that somehow can't keep itself clean?

Who will spread apart my
teeth to help me preen?

The dentist entered
and lit up the crane.

Younger, I left his
office with parachute men
and styrofoam warplanes.

Now his latex fingers
slithered about the
inside of my mouth,
perimeter of my lips.

Through his gloves
I could almost taste those
million dollar fingertips.

In this way I became fixated with
the presence of sensational cylinders
in and round the tissues of my mouth.

...*exactly* like what Freud
and everybody else in the world
is always blathering on about...

When I was in the 6th grade I drew this:

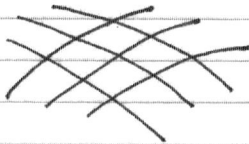

On the wall of my Middle School Cafeteria. When the Principal found out she called in the Art Teacher who took one look @ said this clever little stick looks "Like a Piece of Shit Sol LeWitt!"

I cried No it ain't!, She replied "That's quaint." And then in Marched the janitor to cover the whole thing in STINKY White PAINT!

Two Sure Signs of Depression

Friends,

If you see me walking around
with washboard abs and a loaf
of my own fresh baked bread,
please know that all is not right
inside of the home I call my head.

My Sad School Applications,
In Which I Exempt myself from GREif

Exclusion begins the instant
you can no longer contribute
to what people already say.

So I imagined a box in
which we four must sit;
and — surprise, surprise —
it would have to be
non-quadrangular
in order for me to fit!

It was so stupid, the way their bodies
slowly but literally turned away
from me as they continued to speak.

You would never know it,

But upon occasion I, too, can gleek!

A Frothy Emotional Appeal to God The Mother

Am I not allowed to love
nor obliterated get?

Why is it every time
I held a hand is a time
I would rather forget?

Should I be lowered
into the confines of a
deep dark oubliette?

Yes, but also no - not yet.

Instead,
carry me to bed
pull off my shoes
pat my lumpy head
tuck me in for a snooze.

Then put me beneath the sheet
wherein young men are
transfigured into poet meat.

Then, in the morning,
relieve me of the pain
that prattles on about love being
a thing clicked inside my brain.

Guide me, then, to repair the
mutilation that stole my foreskin.

As a child, I received circumcision
wherein all I wanted was X-Ray Vision.

Not less innervation to make
me mindfuck myself less forgiving
of what my body did opposed to said —
a person unwilling to wed their lover
simply because they're good at giving head.

Please microwave my dense pulpy heart,
nuke it into nachos that are clearly cheesy art.

Burn me like peat beneath a bog,
or else get up off the couch and
feed the fire another log.

"ACAB ACAB ACAB — all cops are hogs."

Birth control, Rand Paul,
and computer speak — I tried
to sneak up on sadness but
then sadness heard the floorboards creak.

She asked, "Would I get an injection
in the pipeline of my vas deferens?"

No, but I will cry crazily
and leave windshield wiper
notes about love and scay-bay-bees.

Forever foam for you like
I've contracted ray-bay-bees.

Be like Russell Edson and
live mirrored sadness joy.

Become a battery squib
whose purpose is to foil —
to foil and annoy!

I haven't felt a spark in years.

So I shuffle my feet,
and grab my keys.

Won't a little static
shock set me free?

Why is it everytime I'm
about to do something big,
I have to stop and pee?

But Bill Burroughs...

For the first time in my life
I have learned that I share
the same writing regimen
as somebody considered
successful — famous —
even legendary in the scene.

And I'll tell you without refrain
that this has done a doozy
on the chemicals inside my brain.

You see, I like it leisurely.
So when I read — no shit —
that Octavia Butler
wrote between the hours
of 2 and 5am (!)
or that Téa Obreht
finished her first novel
by sleeping during the day
and writing through the night
like some wigged out raccoon,
I get to thinking I'm in big trouble.

That's because I'm stubborn
— refuse to set an alarm —
and spend too much money
on pizza and chicken parm.

But Bill Burroughs —

Oh boy Bill Burroughs
woke slightly before 9am
(just like me)
got going around 10am

(just like me)
and then broke
(just like me)
for a "skimpy" lunch
right around noon.

Watch the documentary.

Come 5 o'clock Bill Burroughs
was done for the day.

All full of Dilaudid
& ambiguously gay.

Old Bull Bill, the guy wore
a full suit his whole life yet
called it a disguise, able
somehow never to become
the thing he always
pretended to be.

Insert parentheses,
add question mark.
(Just like me?)

Doggie Dream Poem

I.

I am a dog.

Therefore, I need
to be walked.

I am a dog.

Therefore, I only take
and "bark, bark"
is how I talk.

Indeed, I am a dog
with the habits of a cat —
my love is conditional
and *that is that.*

II.

Hodges the Red Heeler
was a dog for whom I sat
back in the day when
I lived in New Mexico
(Santa Fe).

Hodges Sweet Potato
was this dog's full name
if you must.

Sweet Potato was a nightmare,
but he was also a dog.

And because he was a dog,

like I am a dog, he needed to run
roam and stretch his doggie legs
else he'd go out of his little doggie head.

So I took Hodges
to the lawn in front
of the courthouse
to run with him
as fast as I could.

To do so was in our blood,
our top speed the same —
he with his four legs and
me with my bi-ped frame.

We both panted and then lost our minds
rolling on our backs in a zoomed out
fit of ecstasy right there in the grass.

Hodges, hear me speak:

You were a total nightmare,
but you never bit anybody.

Just barked and growled
and pretended to be an ass.

I know plenty of people
who are total nightmares.

They, too, never bit *anybody* —
just barked and growled
and acted totally crass.

They are good people
and they are good dogs
who stop the squabble

once you realize they're
not actually totally nuts.

Too bad — I think — that we humans can't
discern everything we need to know about
each other simply by smelling each other's butts.

Instead I ask somebody a *perfectly audible question*
and they immediately reply with an extraneous
"What?!"

Man that gets my hackles up,
makes me gruff.

Poem

Teenage thoughts

from a teenage brain:

If you listen to Maroon 5

after *Songs About Jane*,

I cannot respect you,

will call you so many names.

A Nice Little Packet of Five

I.

Sometimes,
I play possession
with depression.

And so get _mad_
when somebody else
tells me they're _sad._

II.

"I want you to read my work
and then kill yourself."

What do I mean?
Why did I write this?

Why did it fly across my brain
trailing banner like a bi-plane?

III.

I'm so square.

Seriously, just look at my hair!

IV.

I've been picking scabs again...

texting, emailing (?!?)

ex-girlfriends...

V.

I wonder:
Would it be better
if I were deader?

Will I be like Lee Krasner
after Jackson Pollock died?

Will I be alright after
a good, long, hard cry?

SAD Poem About Seasons
From the Year I Bought a
SAD Light to Fix My SADness

I do not care what season it is,
I do not give a *FUCK*.

The future advances
toward me like a bullet —

I could stop it but I don't even duck.

I will not be happy in the summer and
at my saddest in early spring.

I will not cry on the winter solstice,
nor fear what January might bring.

No, I will not light my life by the bright white beam
of some Amazon recommended cock ring.

My Refractory Period

I.

I once went down on a girl because
I wanted to prove I am a guy who _cares_
and not just some dude who gets his
and never gives anybody else _theirs._

But it went poorly, unappreciated,
and, worst of all, was totally not hot.

... I was only trying to be polite
by putting my mouth in a place
that doesn't get much light.

But instead had once again got
in my head to act on something
I read in a Reddit thread.

My greatest fear I must now tell:
these poems aren't artful missives
that will simply never sell,
but _doggerel_ — lines of text
ripped right out of incel hell.

II.

Why must men yawp and
women yip every time they cum?

Is the novel of gestures over:
Should we pronounce
it dead and done?

And what has the internet done

to a once virile young buck?

Streaked my eyes with
nectar from a flower plucked?

Transformed me into a
goddamn betacuck?!?

A chicken man who
can only say, "Cluck, Cluck?"

A nice guy who happens
to be down on his luck?

A man married to himself
who suddenly feels stuck?

A scared little boy who
desperately no longer
wishes to give a ____.

A Poem About Nectarines That Ends
With A Brief Defense of Short Kings

Nobody can eat a properly ripe
nectarine without immediately needing
to shower and scrub away the stick.

And nobody can throw a block
of clay without their hands
begging for moisture — a squirt
of lotion — to keep away the "Ick!"

And nobody can wake after a night
of too much sugar and too little sleep
without a canker sore sprouting up inside
their mouth like a gross little freak.

Give it the whole next day
and treat it like a thing for
your tongue to savor.

A canker sore is a rotted piece
of flesh that feels like the
spongy head of a pencil eraser.

Next time this happens,
I will rip it off my cheek
and swallow it like a wart.

As well, people have _got_ to stop
mistreating men who are short.

"The Good Old Days"

On the exterior of a shopping bag
belonging to a store that sells knick-
knacks disguised as bric-a-brac,
I saw a quote:

"The only way to get rid of
temptation is to yield to it."

This quote is used to sell products.

And then in Cimetière du Père Lachaise,
Wilde's Tomb surrounded by thick glass
to keep away the homophobes who,
absent access to a mythic thicc ass,
might tag it with a swastika or two.

It's just — just —

Whenever the world paints me blue,
I think back to when Neo awoke
to the face of Morpheus
(this is actually what I do)
and revealed to his Master
that, in a matter of seconds,
he had learned Kung-Fu.

With the right kind of machine I guess you
could technically make horses out of glue.

That Very Special Night When Glenn Gould Was The Answer To a Clue on Jeopardy! and I Alone Knew It — Very Special

When I, like Glenn Gould,
read or write or watch a film
I always hum along, making
sure nobody is ever around
to hear my silly little song.

And this is easy because
I live alone and my art
is the only thing that would
ever dare replicate the sound
of a friend calling on the phone.

The only difference, then, between I and Glenn
is that he plays the piano and I write.
But also that in 6th grade somebody
threw a football at my head and we
proceeded to engage in the saddest, lamest fight.

But, truthfully, the difference between me and Glenn
is that when I hum I don't ruin the f&*king movie
because I always watch when nobody is around,
maniacally adjusting the sound with each rise
and fall in the cadence of a character's speech,
pausing every so often to scoop into my mouth
another bite of Apple Sauce & Cottage Cheese.

I know it sounds disgusting, but it's actually pretty good,
you've probably never tried it, but I really think you should.

Upon listening to Richard Brautigan
babble on about instant coffee
and then brush his teeth
all while combing his hair:

Why does Richard Brautigan
sound like Kermit the Frog,
that puppet who's been
on Omegle showing off his BGC
instead of appearing on Telly-V
to teach kids their ABC's?

- What does Richard Brautigan
sound like Kermit the Frog

William F. Buckley Jr.: The Solicitor
General of White Privilege

Jerry Garcia finally taught me what
the problem is w/ New England.

It's that the horizon - your horizon -
is constantly above & the center of
your vision. This, too, is the problem
w/ the cities.

Get the horizon below your center every
once and awhile and you won't feel
so stuck you won't - as Most
New Englanders do - think everything
is such a big deal.

"But, COVID we're gettin'
Marriedddddddd!!!"

43

Another poem for Richard Brautigan,
whom with you I have shared
loved instant coffee and
sounded like Kermit the Frog

Friend,

Rejoice!

I can drink
coffee again-èd

But know there was a time
when I couldn't, a time when
I wouldn't, because caffeine
made violent thoughts appear
when they really shouldn't!

Yet I would still do it —
drink the acid coffee addiction
and then hide in my bed
imagining vasoconstriction
phosphene red Avicii's *Levels*
booming in my head.

That's my *brain*
issuing death threats
with the certain scream
of a subway train?

My bodymind arrives at a question:
Shall I change my entire life again?

No, no (There, there).

If I learned one thing from watching sweet Regis,

44

it's that you can always phone a friend or,
if they don't answer, shout out to sweet baby Jesus,
and, if that doesn't work, listen to *Yikes* by the man
who calls himself Ye/Yeezus.

Yet another for Richard B.
In which I fail to redeem him for
I've Never Had It Done So Gently Before,
which, to put it politely, went disastrously

The Massage

Date: 9/5/20
Location: Cape Cod Mall

It was just a massage
— bodywork, in fact —
And though I had my doubts
because sometimes
these places do little more
than throw a sheet
over your body like
a corpse at the morgue,
it turned out to be quite good.

10/10; would recommend to a friend.

Jesus but he instead of
flipping over all of the tables
in the temple he steals
everything and gives it to the
poor. They then call him
"Heist Christ" and Robin
Hood is no more.

Heist Christ

Crack-up

Essays I wanted to
write.

How Raymond Carver taught me to
sweat the details', or, why I'm sad.

Loadie: Who is she? What does she
want?

Jack Kerouac Wished He Were Black: This and
other missteps from great American writers

Aww, freak out: The similarities and
dissimilarities between the shark attacks on
the jersey shore in the sums of 1916 and the
spread of the novel Coronavirus in 2020.

Adam Curitis' You Sly frog:
Or Dos Passos' Dance Across the screen

Neither/Nor: How Soren Kierkegaard's greatest-
work felt out was co-opted by Nazi and these
left us with no other option than a whole
sale rejection of his work

48

Errors in my thinking

Compromise w/ Practical
Practical w/ Center
Center w/ Rational
Rational w/ Practical
Practical w/ Compromise

Ethical w/ Just
Just w/ Religion
Religion w/ God
God w/ Just
Just w/ Ethical

Intelligent w/ Moral
Moral w/ Kind
Kind w/ Generous
Generous w/ Moral
Moral w/ Intelligen

More →

Wise w/ Old
Old w/ Age
Age w/ Happy
Happy w/ Young
Young w/ Old
Old w/ Wise

Complaint w/ Criticism
Criticism w/ "Should"
"Should" w/ "Good"
"Good" w/ Negative
Negative w/ Criticism
Criticism w/ Complain

Pain w/ Meaning
Meaning w/ Wisdom
Wisdom w/ Age
Age w/ Meaning
Meaning w/ Pain

More →

Different w/ Bad ✓
Bad w/ New ✓
New w/ Complex
Complex w/ Bad
Bad w/ Different

Familiar w/ Good
Good w/ understood ✓
understood w/ Quality
Quality w/ Good
Good w/ familiarity

did it.

How To Buy A Home Poem

Adopt Friedmanite austerity.
Decline invitations to brunch.

Forgo gifts to charity.
Consume Cap'N Crunch.

Watch the television.
Entertain all the facts.

Everybody has opinions.
Nobody wants the vax.

Cancel all subscriptions,
except the local paper.

Tucker Carlson in conniptions:

Says it's nbd that Maxwell
pegged Virginia so Epstein
could rape her.

Retreat into yourself,
you want to escape society.

Pull a book off of the shelf:
Davis, Disturbance, Varieties.

How To Buy a Home Poem,
to save money become stranger.

Your only friends are phone videos
that convert laughter into anger.

Open Google Sheets,

since you don't know Excel.

Boss still uses Hotmail,
they can go to Hell.

Pursue new opportunities
under banner of practicality.

Read up on annuities,
dream of different reality.

Seek something simpler.
Try to be productive.

Putting goals onto paper
... feels a bit reductive.

Rewatch *Good Will Hunting*,
know it's not your fault.

Your life is endless punting,
guess you're not John Galt.

Buy yourself some food,
mainly rice & beans.

Friends ask if you're good,
you don't know what they mean.

Explain absent materialism
isn't something fancy.

Just a coping mechanism,
when no money makes you antsy.

Another battle with bureaucracy,
they misspelled your name.

Thought comes to kill yourself
since it's more or less the same.

Headlines says you did it,
you killed the economy.

All frogs say, "Ribbit!"
Isn't that hegemony?

Appointment for a home loan,
tell them you've been good.

"Give a dog a loan bone?"
"No, but wish they could."

Every day feel more dumb
about your student debt.

At least it's still free to cum —
and stifle for an instant the
endless, gnawing regret.

Retreat *further* into yourself,
to save become *even* stranger.

Pull a book off of the shelf,
Austen, Abbey, Northanger.

Have a little breakdown
— a little panic attack.

Need to be more vocal,
like that duck from Aflac.

Attend important protest;
prefer to talk Dothraki.

Biden, Clinton, Kerry
all voted 'Yes' to kill Iraqis.

Wonder about the world
and everybody in it.

Buy an ice cream with a swirl,
"Is there no other way to spin it?"

Draft *How To Buy a Home Poem*,
in which the blessed eat only rice and beans.

Desire *Never Leave Your Home Poem*,
in which it's okay to be blue *and* green.

Alas it's *How To Buy a Home Poem*
written like a set of stilted instructions.

Just wish that I could phone home,
feel medical fetish alien abduction.

Instead, a saucy poetic reduction
about settling the mother feelings.

Written for those staring at the ceiling
without will enough to watch a movie,
nor a father figure to call and explain
that despite the four-year-degree life's
not exactly going all that groovy.

Internet's advice: "If you're willing
to endure some ads you can actually find
some pretty good content on the Fox
Corporation streaming service called "Tubi."

Poem About Blood, Poem About HUD

Were you even there if you didn't wake up
each morning and take three hard swallows
to gauge the throat for any trace of soreness?

Did you not then vehemently wash
your hands with scented soap
just to smell them, and rub your nostrils
along your palm like a rheumy dog?

Folks were eating raw onions like apples
just to confirm that overnight some
thing hadn't entered their bodies
and worked its way into their blood.

And then it became boring as The Department of Housing
and Urban Development is typically abbreviated as "HUD."

A Poem for People With Office Jobs

Show up late, doesn't matter.
Nobody else is there.
Show up late, doesn't matter.
Nobody is left to care.

Show up late, doesn't matter.
Sit at computer and stare.
Show up late, doesn't matter.
Eat lunch; a single Bartlett pear.

Show up late, doesn't matter.
Change all clocks to digital.
Show up late, doesn't matter.
Destroy all seconds, time is killable.

Adjust the heat in winter,
A/C in the summer.

Life contains one "if,"
— hot or cold —
what a stinking bummer.

When I was younger there occurred an evening in my town that most people would say did not occur. Or, if a person accepts that it did occur, they do not accept that the evening occurred in the manner in which I say it occurred. But often the people who do not accept the description of the events (notice I do not say "my description of the events") neither live in my town nor lived in my town during the time in which this evening occurred. Therefore, these people believe falsely because they deny the truth of a time and place in which they — more or less — did not exist.

As for the people who *are* willing to accept the truth of a time and place in which they did not exist, their words always communicate a belief opposed to the denial I discover in their eyes. Their disbelief is revealed to me when I land upon a fact that threatens what is permissible to the limits of their credulity. They seek, I think, to make the matter an instance of their word versus mine. But here I am forced by convention to err, for we are always forced to present every dispute of the truth as a matter of one person's word versus another. It would sound strange if I had written "their word versus word." But that is exactly how it is; their words versus fact, not one account versus another.

Despite this reality, these people always walk away from me insisting inside their heads — privately, alone — that some part of what I have said must be untrue. Not outright false, no, but untrue. They are convinced that in order to provide the story with a flourish, in order to win the respect and adoration as a teller of stories, that I must have stretched some fact a bit too far, or omitted some detail that would reduce my encounter with the extraordinary as none other than a fancy — yet false — self-serving rendition of the once-again always-been ordinary.

Yet what happened that evening is not so unbelievable given that 1) It happened and 2) All people, at some point in their lives, experience an evening of sleeplessness so severe that they forsake the practice entirely for at least one more rotation of the earth's diurnal turn around the sun. In this instance, the inability of the people in my town to fall asleep occurred all at once, for every person, on the same evening.

For those who still, in this final moment, doubt the truth of what I am about to share, know that there exists an outcome in which a fresh deck of cards is shuffled endlessly, across all of time, and so is guaranteed to linger for an instant in precisely the same order in which it began. Know that this story is that outcome. Know that that deck of cards — still stinking of pressed plastic — will someday arrive again exactly where it began. Perfectly ordered, perfectly fair, perfectly random.

What I remember most about that evening is the shared sense of blamelessness. Nobody spoke of sirens, bright lights, a cup of coffee consumed at too late an hour nor a roommate who played the TV too loudly into the night. It mattered not. It mattered not, too, what time we all tried to fall asleep because by 3am we had all accepted that sleep simply would not come.

That is how we all found ourselves out in the streets, for the first time in our lives, without fear and without blame to take or to give. And that may be why all of the businesses, despite the absolute firecracker of human activity, remained closed throughout the entire evening. It seemed, without fear and without blame, people had ceased trying to be productive, ceased trying to get ahead, or to make a profit or put a competitor to shame. We decided instead only to walk among each other and never to speak. More plainly than ever before we each waited for one felt moment to collide with the approaching moment off the next. And that was perfectly okay for the simple, yet powerful, reason that everybody else also felt it to be perfectly ok.

Indeed, I recall walking by a person that evening and recognizing a glimmer of awareness in their eyes. We both knew what was happening was miraculous, that we had a secret to spill but would never tell. What we did instead was look at each other and smile, recognizing in our smiles that everything was normal and that everything would be alright because we felt, collectively, together, that it *would* be alright.

Perhaps some folks were confused by this evening. Perhaps they wondered what was this occurrence that takes place only for a moment across all of time, when things are perfectly ordered, perfectly fair, perfectly shuffled. "What is everybody doing?" they might have said inside their heads. But these were the people, whether by choice or out of necessity, who already wandered the street at this hour. They were not perturbed in the slightest, only momentarily confused, for they had been waiting their whole lives for us to join them and the time had finally come. Soon enough, they felt at-ease with the mass of us suddenly by their sides. Any desire to declare ownership over the hour had been relinquished.

I wondered, briefly: Would the slightest utterance shout out like a thunderclap inside a coffee cup and send the lot of us scattering like roaches?

Our sleeplessness lasted only an evening and the

next day began without the interlude of rest. Across the town tiredness was clear upon the face of every person and hung onto their movements like moss. But, there being no one person more awake than the next, nobody could leverage their better night's rest against another person made defenseless and submissive by a terrible, biological craving for sleep. But, my friends, if this is your first time hearing this story or your fifth, it is here where I need you to listen:

There was forgiveness that next day! And even understanding. And as the sky once again began to darken and the world became quieter for just a while, everybody went home when they were supposed and then went to bed when by their bodies they were told. They slept without flaw, calm as could be. And then, the following day, without a single word on the matter, no proclamation nor battle cry bloodshed eschatological revelation made right by wide-sweeping legislation, everybody in the town fell fast asleep knowing that, through restlessness, their lives had become just slightly more bearable, and so a lot more better — like the first time you felt terrified to write "love" at the end of a letter.

A Poem of Becoming,
for anybody who'd rather Be

My personality is shit
and I cannot change it.

I cannot effect upon
my person-hood the kind
of Copernican Revolution
that Immanuel Kant could.

Indeed, I am tasty wheat —
I am neither interesting nor neat.

Just Fleisch.

Gutted and ground down into
180 pounds of poet meat.

I am too (and you!)
one type of bread,
one type of fruit,
one type of vegetable.

And the joke?

It's affably ineffable &
laughably inexpressible.

Like a button
that is clickable
but also pressable.

To Think is to Stink, A Poem About Animals

I.

Lord,

I don't want to live in a world
where all of the plants are mean!

But I suppose that's what happens
when we rip and shred and
put in a vase everything
beautiful, nice, and green.

II.

My friend once went to N-Y-C
to take in some natural history.

When she arrived at the museum,
she found all of the children gathered
around the animals thought most
mythical, alluring, and fascinating.

These were, in other words,
all of the animals that by
acts and axe of human dint
had vanished, gone kaput,
become extinct.

These were:

Great Auk, Passenger Pigeon,
Mauritian Giant Skink.

Shortly thereafter I heard her speak

something that into my mind
continues to sink:

"This world isn't long," she said,
"for those whom *we*
deem unable to think."

Fear of the Future

I will often read a book
or watch a classic film
and wonder what on
earth I am doing.

Books take countless
forevers to finish and
the characters in old films
never end up screwing.

As of this moment,
I am totally over plot —
the best thing I ever read
being a script about Batman
written by an anonymous bot.

My brother — we joked —
didn't care much about plot either.

Nobody could say for sure, yet still we gibed,
"Matthew reads books middle back
to front topped off by the teaser!"

It seems my brother preferred to know
how everything would end *before*
learning how it all got started.

Kind of like an explorer
who sets out for new lands,
but only those that have
previously been charted.

Ten years since I last saw
my brother hold a book,

the old boy revealed he *would*
skip to the end to sneak a look!

That sly dog cookie crook fool of a took.

He makes me doubt the falsity
within the annals of my family.

Like when my mother tried
crack to "know the enemy."

Was this a joke told
metageneaologically?

Is my family from North Carolina —
or was it Tennessee?

Is it really a peacekeeper who
mixes true with false making
a milieu of frenemies?

I could take solace in a guaranteed future —
meet people at the point of departure.

Wrest and turn upon myself
the bow of that cherubic archer.

Read a book but already know the ending.

Buy everything and only then start spending.

Break everything and only then start bending.

Fight everyone and only then start fending.

Heal everyone and only then start mending.

Win everything and only then start contending.

Secure a love and then live the lines of my life in reverse.

But wait a second...

Love's not a fricken spell, but the lifting of a curse!

I could build backwards to the messages
that both you and I indiscriminately hearted!

We'd be kind of like explorers setting out for new land,
but only one that has been previously charted!

Read this book back to front
and wonder how it all got started.

Esperanto But in English or Portman Teau's
Ponomatopoeic Thedictisauraus for a
More Divergent World

Acidentally — ~~When you pick the wrong punch-~~
~~bowl at one of Ken Kesey's Acid Tests only to real-~~
~~ize there was never a correct punchbowl to begin~~
~~with.~~

Asinine — A particularly attractive rump (man or
woman); a 9 out of 10.

Bloviate — When a lone bovine's ego becomes so
bloated that it forgets its humble Bovinae begin-
nings.

Broil — ~~A boisterous roil; when a pot of water~~
~~begins to boil so ferociously that you can hear it~~
~~from the living room, snapping you out of your for-~~
~~getfulness and permitting you to proctor a goodly~~
~~number of frozen raviolis into its maw.~~

Brevity — Brief moments of levity; a joke, a laugh, a
glance, love.

Divisive — 1) Pertaining to the use of device in
order to tell a story. E.g. Tobias Wolff's utterly odd
story "Bullet in the Brain" about a man who takes
a bullet to the brain and then can't stop muttering/
remembering "short's the best position they is."
More broadly, when you realize something you're
reading is constructed entirely with device and is
born out of some quirky creative writing workshop
exercise.

Eleast-est — When shockingly privileged people
pull rank and try their darndest to prove how much
less privileged they are compared to their shock-
ingly privileged friends.Typically this includes
mentioning the service job they worked one sum-
mer at such and such beachside community.

Friction — ~~1) The feeling you get (hot behind the~~

ears, antsy) when reading a particularly good — or bad — work of fiction indicating either to cancel all plans or take a walk or set it aside and read something else. 2) The force that keeps Great Thinkers from becoming Great Writers; "artistic inertia."

Froggy — What you really feel like in the morning; foggy + groggy.

Habitude — When a person points out an objectively irksome aspect of your behavior in order to help you correct it but instead you become miffed and tell them to piss off only to realize later, in private, that they are right.

Manneurysm — When you're unsure which of your manners to express in a given moment so instead just freeze and your ability to concentrate becomes palsied, droops. Not unrelated to "Syembolism."

Profligacy — When you're so prolific and work so quickly that you sometimes transpose letters but also allow your prolific ability to tarnish the quality of your work (quantity over quality) and so tarnsih your legacy by being too prolific, too accomplished that you don't leave anything for anybody else (E.g. Ben Lerner).

Renunciate — 1) When you state — loud and clear — that you are completely and totally over a situation or somebody and now the whole world knows it. 2) When in the course of such a renunciation you access a lucidity and level of diction typically inaccessible to anybody not engaged in the act of renunciating somebody or something. A new psychedelic state. Fidel Castro hand-waving level aplomb.

Sadisfied — 1) When you must regrettably tell a dear friend "I told you so" but also wish they would just sometimes listen to you so you didn't have to do that! 2) When a sadist is through, finished, done, satiated.

Sould — (No Prononication Possible) When you already know deep down inside (your soul) what it is you ought to do and no way no how cannot shake it yet cannot bring yourself to speak it.

Syembolism — The state of being terminally over-come by symbolism so much so that a figurative blood clot travels to your lungs and you literally die. Cf. Manneurysm.

Additions encouraged below:

Dark Meat

(Fatter, Fuller)

My Old Man Friend

Hello there,
old man sitting
atop my head
fixed to a chair.

Old man whose purpose
is to demonstrate
precisely how much
I do not care.

He has adopted a role.

He is a *dramatis personae*.

But look at his teeth —
many lacunae.

His role:
Old Man Fixed to
a Chair Who Appears
as Young Man with
Full Head of Hair.

That is, a young man
— very self-aware —
despite the presence
of old man who
does not care.

His visage is the
opposite of an acid trip.

His expression forever
fixed with stiff upper lip.

Muttering constantly
that the world needs
to "get a grip."

When others are sad,
it is he who acts surprised.

When others shed tears,
it is he who never cries.

Sure,
It might occur to shatter this mirage
but, truthfully, he possesses no hammer
— the requisite equipage.

No, he cannot beat
his shadow a bloody red.

And I cannot kill the old man
who sits in a chair fixed
to the top of my head.

For his behavior is a gag,
it has become a bit.

Folks count on him!
He can express <u>no emotion</u>
— they rely on it!

Sometimes, people will ask
his opinion on something,
a subject about which they
know he cares, a subject
over which any other person
might cry.

But he doesn't react.

He shows no emotion.
And this raises people up.
Gets them going.
Gets them high.

They begin to admire him,
to appreciate him more.
His ability to show no emotion —
it is what they adore.

Eventually, they begin to say he has "no soul."

This both terrifies and excites him.

What, then, exists inside this hole?

Eventually he begins to conflate honesty, integrity,
and character with a lack of feeling.

If his heart were a room, the paint upon the walls
would be peeling.

Still, he feels good about his role.

Still more, he feels good about his purpose.

Life is but a dream and emotion is worthless!

But then, something terrible happens, it makes him
feel like a child.

He begins to feel so happy about his life that he
wants to smile.

But he cannot smile, he does not dare,

For then he wouldn't be
Old Man Fixed to Chair Who
Appears as Young Man
with Full Head of Hair.

If he smiled, he would no longer have a role,
he would no longer have emptiness
in the space where should be his soul.

And he has come to love this role,
to show no emotion and set them at ease.

The world has rules, damn it!

A man can't just do whatever he damn well please!

But it feels so *good* that he wants to tell!!!

And then he realizes he is trapped,
that by showing no emotion, he
has created his own private hell.

He can only show he cares by not caring;
when others turn away from the abyss,
it is he who must go on staring.

He becomes like a person who affects a funny voice.

But he has done it for so long that he no longer has
a choice.

He walks around in nobody's shoes but his own.

He exists in a funny voice. He is, in the plainest,
most straightforward way,
terribly sad, terribly alone.

He wants to laugh. He wants to smile. He seeks
ways in which
he can recapture his inner child.

But he has made a performance
out of staying forever composed.

He is a man who shows no emotion
even when he is supposed.

A human door that is open,
with a sign that says "closed."

8th Grade,
Maybe 7th,
Definitely 10th

I.

In 8th grade — maybe 7th —
I stood by myself in the gym
like many other children
who stand by themselves
in the gym for what seems
an interminable fire drill
but cannot be whatsoever
practice for the existence
of any kind of fire because
it makes absolutely zero sense
to be gathered together
— all we children —
right there in the gymnasium,
little prepubescent piles
of bright burning magnesium.

II.

In 8th grade — maybe 7th —
I wore to school a number fifty-three
orange and blue Mets jersey tee.

It is the same day as
the false fire drill memory
but also ask somebody
who went to Woodstock
if they saw Jimi Hendrix play
and if they 'Yes' call bullshit
and tell them, "No way!"

He played last, everybody had left,
it was morning on a Monday.

So the one kid looked to the other,
saw my T-shirt, and said: "Let's go
call him a 'motherfucker.'"

"But Billy Wagner is good,"
the other boy refrained, knowing
nothing makes a person sound
more insane than falsely claiming
a future hall-of-fame ball player
to be lame.

And thank god. Thank god this
other boy had the mind to tell
this angry boy to abstain —
or else I might have fainted,
like when I went down
face to the floor from
formaldehyde fumes
flowing off a DIY
dissection deer brain.

III.

Eight years later I learned
I had no idea how to pronounce
Wagner, nor a thing about Twelve Tone,
Das Rheingold or Tristan and Isolde.

Then I watched Stephen Fry
beg and cry as he tried to laugh
and moralize us into a separation
of Wagner's music from this Hitler guy.

I don't know. It's a strange kind of brand.
Like those Fairfield County wasps who
wander the world proselytizing for Ayn Rand.

IV.

In 10th grade a friend used
YouTube as an aid to masturbation.
He searched for:
"Girls in tight ass jeans," "Sexy nerds,"
as well as "mud wrestling."

Clean.

How wholesome and heart-warming
can a person's perversity be?

My friend slid his hand
down his pants because
he liked what he see.

Clean.

Then of course there was the kid
who came into his hand and
took a taste just because it was free.

Clean.

An apple fell far from the tree
and somebody labeled it "Depravity."

Clean.

Later, this same friend
lent a pair of boxers to me.

We had just finished swimming.

They were tight.
Holdovers from when
we were boys with slight
hips and slender legs.
Now a gigantic hole
had been torn
through the front,
where, I must assume,
his dick and balls had
come bursting through.

His brother kept a massive bag
of condoms hidden in his room.

He passed them out
to us like poker chips,
but what were we to bet?

A whole bag but
not a single Trojan.

This left me quite perplexed.

Had I been bluffing,
played my hand a little
too close to my chest?

Just another prophylactic,
thrown in with all the rest.

A Meditation for Obsessive Compulsives Who Are Fearful They Will One Day Have Pedophillic Thoughts

George Eliot said sane people
do as their neighbors do
so that if any lunatics are
at-large we might know them
and then fly the coop.

But really just avoid them —
and probably cease to wave.

There being no secret more shocking
— nothing more depraved —
than to learn of the man
who had a terabyte of child porn
on his computer saved.

In order to heal, the public required
a picture of this _Homo economicus'_ dome.

(We all know exactly what looks like
the face of a man who keeps
pictures of "cum covered infants"
in a Dropbox folder on this phone)

But a picture is necessary for closure,
it is _essential_ to see the faults of
a face made worse by flashbulb exposure.

And it it weren't?
If it were pretty?

— Well that'd be kind of shitty.

But also pretty would perplex us.

Evil's s'pposed to be poor and ugly,
not drive a black Lexus.

Jeffrey Dahmer scored
a Netflix series because
he was hot.

Seven men laid down
their lives because they
fancied Aileen Wuornos a thot.

Can I or can I not —

rejoice for he had a face
full of wens and divots,
plus patchy facial scruff
Albumin puff highlighting
the pimple-torn rivets.

Hark! Some people suffer from
an unfortunate condition,
in which worry about certain
thoughts cry out of their
minds like mewing kittens.

It keeps them afraid longer
than anybody should be,
just like they were a fraidy cat
stuck way up high upon a
branch of their genealogy tree.

But I am normal

~ *totally cool* ~
and

~ worry free ~

Young.

so young

forever _gorgeous_

WILD & ME.

The Way Meditation Works

I resumed a regimen
and learned a lesson.

By the bell felt bad and tough.

Stood over my dis-built body —
are two-hundred and six
sticks really enough?

A squirrel lives inside me
digging for memories
that won't shut up.

Like Ocracoke Samples
of Rocky Road Fudge.

And questions, like:

How do I un-gunk the slime
of my latest grudge?

Why by opening my throat
to snake a drain of latest sludge.

Luden's Cherry Red Cough Drops
plunked down a pipe caked
with shaving cream
soap saliva and blood.

In my mind I'm like:

Is this Chris Farley's mythic white mud?

Toothpaste mixed with mucus

— Chris says he said crud.

John Donne squished a flea
and never penned a single dud.

And Guy La Fille, well, he meditated
to be free and therein lies the rub.

Some days I give myself
the same look as the refrigerator
when I search its guts for grub.

Suppose I am hungry for meaning —
a philosophical club.

Or else something sweeter, like
a packet of pharmacological Stevia.

My insides are rotting from the
combination of some New Age
strain of trichinosis and tularemia.

In the 3rd grade the school sent
around a letter saying Zach Kavalski
had developed leukemia.

I once had to be tested for sickle cell anemia.

That same day I shot dead a squirrel
with a twelve hundred foot
per second pellet gun.

That the same winter,
I memorized the glass-lined
words of Old Latrobe just for fun.

By 2017 I swore off drink;

by 2022 I swore off being done.

There are no permanent solutions
to temporary problems.

What is being handed a set of equations
without the information required to solve them?

The Treadmill Marathon World Record Holder
once sat across from me and ate an entire
apple up to, and including, the core.

My childhood questions persist:

If I never had anything to start,
how can I have some more?

I make the same mistakes like:
Pennywise and a Dollar Poor.

I beg for permanence when
I *already promised* not to ask
for anything anymore.

I try the handle when I *already*
shut those lights, drew those curtains,
closed that door.

I do dumb shit!

Like ruin a perfectly good poem
by concluding it with the totally
uncalled for pronouncement of
the word "Whore."

STOP!

Please leave your
Mood at
the
door

↓

I just can't
take it
anymore!

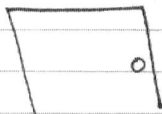

Wintertime New England, 2002

I reckon bins of twizzlers
and a Dreamcast stashed
behind the tree.

Tell me, Guillaume Apollionaire,
how fast _does_ move technology?

Quizzical millennials shout at
children by capitalizing:
"TOWER TWO, DUMMY!"

You beautiful man with shrapnel wrap
about your head and hair.

волосы волосы —
like you-just-don't-care.

Did-ya hear what happened?

Did-ya hear what occurred?

People planes and sheafs of paper
falling from the sky like windowed birds.

I didn't pick my nose!

What you mistook for boogers
was really Cheez-It gunk
stuck up in my gums.

All _I_ did was index it from one place
in my mouth over to my tongue.

Personally, I saw more people cry when

baby Kennedy died than when into the
twin towers two respective planes did fly.

In Middletown, Connecticut —
Postcard in book I found tucked.

Old style, a man to his lover,
1943 "Never forget."

I don't know about you,
but I *cannot believe*
every single person
on this planet once existed
without a single regret.

I Will Regret This

My mother grew up

so lonely that she suffered

the pain of childbirth

— three times —

so as not to suffer

the pain of loneliness

instead.

Imagine this taking place
inside your head.

NO TITLE

My friend and I spent
a day with all the cinema
of Harmony Kyrsten
Korine Sinema.

When were done (and just for fun)
we went and grabbed my daddy's loaded gun.

We then quickly put it back,
put on different hats
(took a different tack)
began writing over and over
again that watching *Gummo*
is like ~~herding~~ cats.
hurting.

WRITTEN, CROSS OUT HERDING, WRITE HURTING, WRITE THIS FINISHED POEM ALL
OVER PAPER.ALREADY DONE, OVERLAY EDITS ONTO OTHER VERSION,

PALIMPSEST?

hurting cats.

Men Are Messed Up

Why like I five
auto-erotic
asphyixi-eye?

Appeal.

He got off on female
tennis player grunts —
stabbed his parents

to death.

Suppose it has to do

with breath.

Suppose it feels good when

there's nothing left.

I get walloped.

I get in bed.

All Jesse & Jane

spoon + spoon

percolating in
the pockets that
comprise my brain.

Why is it young men insist
on showing young women

films that imply their pain is
a head filled not with sunshine
but the heaviest, wettest rain?

We know these men
who seek to demonstrate,
by the end of the first date,
just how much they are capable
of love — and by love, I mean hate.

ART FRIEND

My art friend fancies themselves
special as a snowflake made not
by nature but by paper — complete
only after several hundred snips.

Okay, friend-o.

But when your hair needs holding,
don't forget whose hands perform
the work of countless clips.

And when your tale needs tolding,
remember who made a mouth
where before there were only lips.

Grift me lines like,
"When life hands you
lemons make beef stew."

Okay weirdo —
I make learned references too:
"I am Nobody, Who are you?"

Existers on the fringe.

Hold backers on the lam.

Of a sudden we go: bam, bam.

A single explosion drains the
most masculine mannered man.

A single explosion makes us sweat
the threat of the exclusion clan.

My friend, though, gave me an excessive lesson
about divisive missives, said alternate definitions
do wherein the masses become dismissive.

Told me, too, that all a work needs said
can be cut down to the title for a book never
to be written let alone printed and read.

As for people, I argued it is
unquestionably the same.

For I have never yet met
a person more interesting
than one whose life is full
of Noch Nicht, Not Yet.

To my art friend I lost a bet,
had to get a dictum tattooed
across my chest one million times
worse than "No Ragrets."

We built a romance of a Black Sun Sect.

We love and hide from the
world like cozy little insects.

They left my brain *devastated*
when I felt for the first time
proud of the things to which
I masturbated.

My art friend approaches
places a hand over my mouth
and tells me to shoosh.

Our days live and die so *strangely* —

at night fall asleep together
watching reruns of
The Mighty Boosh.

Some say we need boundaries,
I say, "What would be the use?"

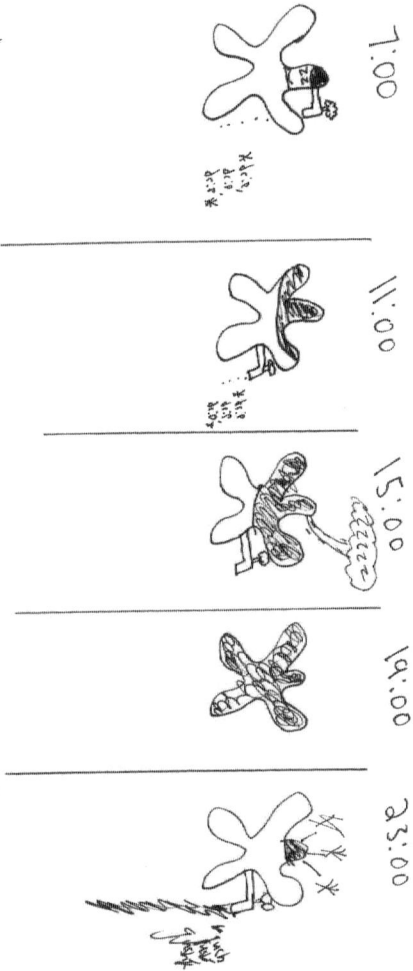

A Day In the Life of Everybody

7:00   11:00   15:00   19:00   23:00

🔲 = cortisol/
Stress juice

*Dreams come from the rapid outrush of-
Stress juid zoom; through the brain Sluice*

<u>*Upon Investigation the 50th (Platinum)*</u>

I crave calm and affirmation
the way the standard meter
craves its *mesure*—
the literal rod of platinum in Paris.

Otherwise, how can I not feel
all the time the way a meter
must feel all the time:

            a little
off.

Upon Investigation the 50th (Gold)

When Pharaoh died,
so did his forearm.

Does this mean I need a
touchstone for my thoughts
to know when they are gold?

A person by my side whose hand
I can unconditionally hold?

A lady with decency enough
to walk me in the park
and then grip my hair —
hard — at night
in the dark?

*A poem about two cisgendered heterosexual people
who have no sexual experiences other than their own
cisgendered heterosexual experiences*

His girlfriend is a woman.
And though she be a woman,
she does not know what it is like
to be with a woman.

Her boyfriend is a man.
And though he be a man,
he does not know what it is like
to be with a man.

So perhaps this is their problem.

Or perhaps not.

I mean, it could be their problem.

But I suppose they will have to discover
if it is possible to please one another
without first learning how to please
themselves; without encountering a body
that is both theirs and not their own.

To learn what they like...
without being shown.

The First Poem in My Poem Book

I.

My brother came to Buddhism
as a last result, when he said
he did not know for what he had
left to live.

Spoke into the phone
a word like "Anhedonia,"
which is codeword for
"It was nice to know ya."

Sometimes, I get so *miffed* at all
the shit everybody wants to show ya.

II.

I read a book that said it is
impossible to see the world
in any other way than
through ignorance.

We see and understand
only by and through
our misunderstanding.

To see at all is to misunderstand.

I used to adore
syllogisms such as this
until I realized my
body is often nothing
more than something
that needs to take a piss.

In some ways, I have aged into
a magician who has revealed
the secret behind all of their tricks.

How did it happen so soon?

At 29 I have I become so tired
of concepts and intellection
disguised as romantic exploits
and brilliant new erections.

III.

In this book a man became spooked
by the sight of a mountain.

Its crooked peak appeared to him before dawn,
before he could let out one of those wakey-wakey
yawns.

In life I am spooked by the words my brother
speaks.

That book was *The Dharma Bums.*

This book is *180 Pounds of Poet Meat.*

IV.

The mountain did not move
and yet it snuck up on him still.

And so my brother came
to Buddhism when death
ceased to sound scary or shrill.

He simply sent it an invitation,
polite enough to say — a heads up,
a little text, an "I'm on my way."

My mother was so lonely that she had
three children and suffered the pain of
childbirth three times so as not to
suffer the pain of ~~childbirthloneliness~~
instead and the best way for me to
describe it to myself is that having a
child is ~~such like~~ a version of a
haircut and the more children you have
the more times your soul is split but
in a good way I guess because
analogies aren't perfect otherwise they
wouldn't be analogies. And my mom and I
Voldemort but we don't get along
well because I'm one to return fire
and get frustrated when nobody ever
believes me that my mom is innocent
and people should stop complaining about
their moms because I have real gripes
here like the way she's been ~~talking~~
about her will and about her story
for 10+ years now and how she's
always threatening to sell the house in
North Carolina and hit the road even
though all I want is nothing but
someone to advise like a mentor or
sort of someone who in order to cope
with the trauma of their own life
doesn't bury up their head in TV
news and magazines and who will

THE START OR THE GRILL

I only found out about the start of the
grill years later when the numbers my
stepdad had been keeping on it were discovered
in a desk drawer. The numbers were simple tallies
indicating the affirmative and nothing like dates
or qualifications, just numbers. two categories:
turned on (as in lit the grill) and used (as in
used the grill to cook some type of meat). Though
it was unclear when he began or ended his
record keeping. I had cause to dear kest
and my brother Kevin came in first with
something like 95 uses. My stepdad doing
anything of this sort was so out of
Character that I had to rethink everything
I knew about him and so wondered what
else he kept numbers on.

The Great White Conflation

I am white.

Therefore, I conflate
economic exploitation
with racial discrimination.

AND

If I don't soon learn
the difference,
I'm going to kill
many more people
than I already have.

I do not joke, I do not blave;
so go the internecine squabbles
of we class warfare knaves.

Poem About A Symphony (And Suicide!)

2017: A symphony with a friend.
First Shostakovich then the
great Ludwig van Beethoven.

Friend yearned to lean beyond
the edge of the mezzanine.

Why?

Because she'd forgotten
what Kierkegaard wrote
about Mozart, *The Marriage
of Figaro* und *Die Zauberflöte*.

Allegedly, the best place to be
during a symphony is neither
way up high nor on the floor,
but just outside the auditorium
on the other side of the door.

Instead we descended to the front row:
Like a Dodgers game 7th inning
everybody gone LA down 10-0.

I wore radiant shoes that
hideoused off my feet —
tips of the laces torn to bits.
Frayed where once was protection
of cheap plastic aglets.

Next, the lead violinist bursts a string.

She pretends to go on fiddling
so as not to alert those up high

— but not beyond the door —
that the strings of her Amati
have been reduced by one
to three from four.

In fact, she plays more
vigorously than before —
spit flying from her lips
and onto the score.

From the lobby Søren Kierkegaard
would've missed the whole thing —
nervous wreck, anxious Dane
living and dying on the wings
of philosophizing.

Our man just needed somebody
to explain to him that even when things
begin to go terribly wrong,
all is not lost if you're able
to just fake it until you make it,
oder "Wie sagst du auf Dänisch
'Willing to play along?'"

A moment of extreme doubt:

[Even Page followed by two whole blank pages].

August 2021

Years after Pascal's Pensée 270 but
Before Ronald Bronstein's Frownland

I express myself
and communicate
in exactly the same way.

This fact is responsible
for every complication
I have experienced heretofore.

What I am trying to express
is constantly at odds with
what I am trying to communicate.

And

What I am trying to communicate
is constantly at odds with
what I am trying to express.

It's like I'm

.

.

.

boring
a
hole

.

.

.

deep into the ground
and all around
piles of dirt

.

.

.

keep

.

.

.

trickling

.

.

.

down

.

.

.

.

.

.

.

What a difference a day makes

What a difference a day makes —
I believed that until this morning,
which is when I recalled
a poem about a young man
who encounters an old man
at a hardware store and
asks him — the old man —
if he has read the complete
works of Emily Dickinson.

The point of the poem, I suppose,
is to help the reader realize
— while engaging with art —
that endless & supreme engagement
with art grants neither endless
nor supreme satisfaction
— nor contentment —
nor any of the other things
we are supposed to feel
at any one time or another.

The poem, like a paradox,
asserts itself in the world
while undercutting itself
in the same instant.

Indeed, it has "Cut off
the branch upon which
it was sitting."

The poem talks down
to itself the way a twenty-year-old
talks down to themselves when they
meet a man who works with his hands,

or else one of those gnats who pester
college students about their plans.

And what about me?
"This isn't poetry!" I think,
but then go red in the face
for making such a stink.

Why cull? Why say what belongs?

Why say what does not?

Why have peace against twice true paradox?

Make me like Randall after Big Nurse's shock.

Roving, babbling, suffocating

Wondering Peace Chief —

PEACE OR PARADOX?!?

"You know, I would have liked to curate a Philosophical work that... sized entitled

"You know, I would
have liked to curate
a Philosophical work
that consist of
jokes. Wittge...

...obviously
I squeezed too tight
and the bar slipped
out of my hands and

My life was like...

Poem Upon Realizing Why I Can't Take Myself Seriously In My Hometown

Everybody is living
like they forgot what
they were doing.

And in order to remember
what they were doing,
they return to the spot
where once was the
thought they were chewing.

But on the way back

they
      cross
            paths

with a version of themselves,
just as Oedipus crossed paths
with a version of himself
— *his father* —
when he fled Corinth
to spare his blood
the violence of fate
but then splintered
the skull of his papa
into the flesh of
papa's brain since
self-surety is simply
confidence that permits
fists to fly without refrain.

Oedipus played himself —
just like every time I lose

at any type of game

I lash out!

Repress, Swallow, Internalize
my angry hippo pain.

Tell me:

Where is the spot upon which I stood before?

That unfortunate moment in my life
when I uttered, "Maggie's such a whore."

I make one mistake (or several)
and get all a tither.

I play Rock, Paper with my past
and always pick Scissors.

I'm not so sure of myself anymore.

It's not *my* path
to let this second self
(*my father!*) pass.

But everything's just fine —
because — duh! —
I realized in life there exists
 — Rock, Paper, Scissors —
more than just three stupid silly signs...

Knives Scare Me, Lessen Pain

Knives scare me
because they're sharp.

I might get the notion
to make one meet my skin.

But my professor said
he's afraid of handling
a straight line because
(theoretically) it's "Even
more than razor thin."

My professor said this when I was younger,
before I ever had such a notion,
nor could even remember, but
then I felt relieved, let out a laugh
and breathed and so today I'll
do the same not because I want
to play some silly rhyme game
but because knives scare me and
his words really do lessen my pain.

Once upon a time I couldn't

Once upon a time I couldn't watch
films that depicted suicide because
big scary Babadook mean monkee
lurked behind every corner bearing
likeness to a winter coat or filly foal —
a _scarier_ hour never wasted there.

You see suicide would pop-up out
of a book and ruin my day like
some grouch in the checkout line,
or a big ol' truck raised up spewing
balls black smokestack breath
all over you and your family
downtown lipping froyo.

Or, or —

When somebody says your new haircut
made me look like the villain from
a TV show they've been watching,
but that not another person in this
entire room has seen and you go home
and learn that they were wrong,
that I look nothing like this evil oil baron
but everybody has already laughed
because people always laugh and
the feelings already felt and I
hate this person for their Whoville haircut —
what a nut!

I just want to say
that I was trying
to have an okay day.

Go easy on me.

Makes-me-sad.

Still, day after day suicide would appear
out from words when my eyes would slide
to form letter combos out of S's and C's
and I's and -ide's.

Always -ide's.

I would bifurcate language,
chop it to bits and make a monster
where before there was just a Magikarp.

In fact, I got so good at knowing
when a suicide was coming
that somebody would walk up to me
on the street and begin to tell me a story
in which I had the opportunity to guess
the ending, how it all concluded.

Next, I had to act like it wasn't obvious
that a person would take their own life.

No —
no plans, nor plotting, nor
dates upon the wall.

Nothing other than unprecedented
reverence for the power of a single
thought to blot out my light and
spread schemer across my life
thick and opaque as any loxy bagel.

My friends,

Brain chemistry could drop you
at any instant and then how are
you going to keep a fiddle-headed
parasite from sprouting out your
eye so horse hair it makes you cry?

How cruel, then, in those days,
to have worked in a movie theater
where films would play inside my office
and where, for months on end, I had
to observe Woody Harrelson tenderly
blow out his brains in that doting,
romantic way only Hollywood knows how.

In those days, too, my nose would twitch
like the fingers of a chimpanzee
trying to turn the buttons on a typewriter
into the next Great American Novel.

But I couldn't quit, I couldn't stop
because I hadn't enough money
and wanted so badly to live
a life that I cared about
but a life — nevertheless —
that did not care about me.

I said, a life. I cared about.
But a life. That did not.
Care about me.

My brain was coffee
~ steamed ~
to a thousand degrees.

Eventually I learned to
~ chill out ~

but also

started living

caffeine free.

Realized it's better to shout out in glee
than to be sad and go down in history.

I Hate My Height and Weight,
I Treat Myself Like A Piece of Freight

I know a rich girl who takes Vyvanse
because she binge eats.

In place of food, she is prescribed pills.

This stays the worry
she feels about her weight.

But Vyvanse makes a person
lethargic, sedentary —
so far as solutions go
she says, "It's not too great."

When he was younger,
my brother struggled
with worry and with weight.

I imagine him before a mirror —
all he sees is a piece of freight.

But with time came height
and with height a hitch.
My brother developed a curve
in his spine, the kind of
scratch you just can't itch.

Then, in 2016, while doing
seven and a half
of a suspended fifteen,
my brother got ahold of
Dimethyltryptamine.

This selfsame spine,

the one with the hitch,
became an ouroboros ring,
encircled him like a ritual witch.

And when it finally snapped,
when the circle was broken,
it neither hissed nor cried
but rang out like a mario token.

He described it to me,
the way the metal would sing,
it shattered his compulsions
but only for as long as lasts
the song of a pointed brass
tinggggggggggggggg.

II.

I wrote this poem to share
that my brother would also
like to take Vyvanse to
control his compulsivity.

But in prison a person
isn't allowed to do things
you and I do normally.

There is a girl —
she is rich.

There is my brother —
spine with a hitch.

There is the world —
not right for those with
with the wrong weight
as well as the wrong height.

Nor is it really either for
people who aren't white.

But who am I to talk about people?

I'm just a person bent on uncovering the Ponzi scheme
that was the Magazine Drive and The Cult of the Weepul.

*POOR PEOPLE'S DREAM POEM (FOR POOR PEOPLE ONLY)

It will never not be a dream of mine that upon
departing a rental — this my latest — without the
slightest sign of wear & tear no trace of my exis-
tence about the house nor on the floor...let alone
hanta droppings from a mouse snuck in through an
open door, that they, my landlord, will take
hold of my shoulder — no, my elbow — as I de-
scend into the driver's seat of my car one leg in one
leg out split between two lives like a wishbone and
speak, hand to my elbow beat of my heart, like Ni-
etzsche to the horse that lay flayed before the cart:

"Poor People! You have been such a wonderful
tenant these past ten years that the only
way I can possibly think of repaying you is, well, by
literally repaying you."

I say nothing, speak elliptically.

"Indeed, Poor Person, I have stashed away all of
your rent these past ten years and am now return-
ing it to you — with interest, with COLA — as you
go on your way to begin your new life."

"..."

"You see, Poor Person, the truth is I never really
needed your rent in the first place. I am sorry only
to be telling you this now, at the absolute final
moment of your departure and after you have spent
these past ten years struggling to deliver me the
correct sum each month, planning your whole life
by this sum, and ensuring (how very quaint) that

I always received this sum the night before the
1st of each month so that you could claim, in any
imaginary future dispute, never to be late with rent
but always early. You did this because you imagine
it might go a long way in my willingness to show
you not quite mercy nor not quite compassion but
something like sympathy, for I am often guided by
this want to identify with the person upon whom
I decide to loosen my grip. If I don't see a bit of
myself in them, then I retreat into the letter of the
law, their humanity something I pretend never to
have saw."

"..."

"What I really need you to understand, Poor Per-
son, is that from 19__ onward my parents instilled
in me not only a self-effacing pride in my individu-
ality, but a thoughtless subscription to the doctrine
of individualism that would have me take the clas-
sical ideas of liberty, equality, and fraternity and
effect with them a double exposure upon myself,
combining this liberalism with capitalism to birth a
neo-liberalism and make of myself an entrepreneur,
my entire being a little economy, a world market
unto myself. In that way, I could solve *my* ills just as
the market might solve the world's ills — a delicate
touch is all that is needed; a careful stimulation and
expertly-timed inflow of capital.You see, Poor Per-
son, I was raised to believe unfailingly in nameless,
shapeless progress and never to have something as
silly as a crisis of confidence.

"..."

"What aspects of myself could I cure by making
a profit off of them, what world suffering could

131

be healed by incentivizing somebody to make a little money? For people will inevitably do good, won't they, if it is profitable to do good? The world dream, my dear Poor Person, was that we could turn loose the profit motive on things like compassion, care, aid, health, illness, law. But what actually happened is that we made so many excess guns and ammonium nitrate that we had to sell advanced military equipment to police departments and private citizens and then grow oodles of corn — the crop, ironically, that we learned to grow from the natives in order to save our lives — and then made so much of it that we couldn't possibly *eat* all of it so we had to be told to drink its syrup in order not to watch the whole thing go "Ka-boom!""

"..."

"Now we are living with literal tons of folks who think pride lies in an A-K and a Big Gulp from the Speedway. And when you mention this, when you suss it out to show them their ways, they become even more full of pride because you notice, you care, you *see*. And that's all they wanted, to do a little trick with their bike or a cartwheel and wait for Mom and Dad to see, wait for them to yell out, across the playground, "Good job, honey! Keep going!""

"..."

"It's the apathetic misanthropic desire to have your whining shushed and your 'look-what-I-can-do' watched and watched and watched and good job'd and good job'd and a you're not the boss of me and a you're not the boss of me and a you're not my mommy and a you're not my daddy and a says why and says who and a nah nah nah boo boo stick your head in doo doo, but with guns and hate and confidence disguised as conviction and self-reflection. Every infant, I have come to realize, will eventually smear itself in shit only to stare up out of the crib at their parents in goofy dumb shiny dewy newborn satisfaction."

"..."

"What is worse than all of that, and what matters to you most, is that my parents and my peers and society writ large made me this way! I know it all sounds so anguish pearish — passive, determined — the way I have a lust for alienation, reification, and commodity fetishization of anybody at any time on my quest for accumulation. As a teenager, it made me sick with want — stuck together the pages of the econo-pornography magazine that was my life, but now I am an adult, the stain is set in my sheets, the stain that is my self and the things I believe and the way in which I behave. I could say I am this way because of the system, but that would only serve my purpose of making it all the more distant."

"..."

"So when I met you, Poor Person, I could conceive of no other way in which to interact. You and I, we were bound to transact. I must treat you as subject made object involved in the exchange of objects made subjects. The only consolation I can offer is to tell you it isn't personal in the slightest, it has absolutely nothing to do with you, if that makes it any better, if that covers your wounds with healthy green goo.

"..."

"Why was it inevitable? Because I own the land on which you happen to exist and for which you must pay me (who so happened to get here first) money in order to continue to exist. You do this through your labor, which eats up your time, and provides me with more money — money that eats up your time and also further solidifies my ownership over said land and increases the need for you to earn more money through your labor to pay for the land that I own and upon which you must live. And that's where they got you. For you must live, mustn't you? After all, here you are, arriven, with a body that occupies space and a brain that is constantly aware of this fact. It's exactly where healthcare gets you too — same as every other business that makes its work from getting money out of the default state of every human being on earth — the default state of existence."

"..."

"But I cannot stop there, Poor Person, even though you want me to. Even though I have gone on longer than a Karamazov, even though your patience wears thin at all these terms I bandy about and this framework that offers us a glimpse into a different way to relate to one another. Because I must tell you that I have not stopped myself — I who am no bank executive, nor billionaire, nor paid politician — I have not stopped myself in the moments when it mattered because I shirked the responsibility — the individual responsibility — can you believe I am now once again falling back on this notion of individual responsibility as a solution to the very thing an overemphasis on individual responsibility created in the first place! Can you really believe it?!?!"

"It's so pesky! This notion of personal responsibil-
ity, which, believe you me, *DOES* detract from the
fact that only a few hundred select individuals and
entities are responsible for much of the harm in the
world today, but I — me, an individual! — have also
not stopped myself in the moments when it could
have mattered. When given the option to take a
little more off the top for myself I have done it in
each and every instance, with the failed belief that
if I don't do it, then somebody else will. For me the
fear of opportunity lost always outweighed the joy
of opportunity taken."

*Here, my landlord pauses for a few extended mo-
ments to breath and swallow spit that has indubi-
tably pooled inside of their mouth. Their breathing
has quickened as their body demands more air than
their lungs can supply. Oratorically speaking, they
are approaching their VO2 threshold. The decreased
supply of oxygen to their brain puts them at risk for
triggering a stress response in their genes that might
permit a latent mental health disorder to, for a lack
of proper clinical terminology, push its way right out
of its shell. I remain aghast yet curious. After all,
they own me.*

"And then as I was saying before, as the value of my
land increases — because of your money — I begin
to feel justified asking you for more money; money
you must obtain by either increasing the value of
your labor (aka the value placed upon your body
performing particularly specialized motions across
a shorter period of time) or else by selling more
of your labor (the value of your body performing
particularly common motions but across a longer

period of time). Time of which you are allotted only a certain amount by dint of the standard work week. Interesting, isn't it, how time has been turned into a chart of 365 squares filed away by years — systematized to make for a predictable product? But where does this value come from, where? The big green bomb invisible hand spirit living way up in the sky? Heck, Poor Person, these enfranchising terms I'm using aren't even your terms! You are as equally powerless over their meaning as you are over the determination regarding the value of your labor! Mostly, they work only to provide you with the ability to describe your problem, but none of the tools required to fix it."

"..."

"By now I am sure you also recall I own multiple properties, in multiple states. I told you as much when you moved in because my immense privilege sometimes comes blurting out of my mouth like leaky Lay's. And my expenses — my expenses, lol! — I pay them by drawing down on my enormous IRA that simply *took off* after the loosening of financial regulations in the 1980s, a full poor person number of years before you were even born!"

"..."

"Oh, Poor People Person, I don't even have mortgage payments anymore and I just realized your name literally contains the word "Poo!" All of my properties have been in my family for years and have only appreciated enormously in value. I never even bore any of the risk required to buy them. I just use their equity to access new loans that I use to buy more properties — properties I devalue when tax time comes so I can lower the amount I must pay and on and on we go turning and turning and turning in that widening gyre hahahaha."

"..."

"My capital accumulation spans generations! Your piddly ten years — tops — of savings cannot compete with the extralegal effort of hundreds of my ancestors. You've saved $20,000 for a down payment? Cute. Now give me everything you have and settle in for the next fifty years, you knave. My ancestors? I haven't told you about them? They are the ones I unwittingly boast about having been in America "forever" by which I only mean the 17th and 18th centuries. Don't give me that look. Forever can mean however many years I intend. It isn't awkward for me to share the surname with countless buildings and streets that spread out all across indigenous land!"

"..."

"Oh, Poor Person! All I've been doing these past number of poor person years is chucking your checks into my savings account. In fact, I don't even see your checks nor look at them to make sure they're made out for the correct amount, I just pass them along to my bookkeeper and trust that they clear because you're so good. You really are so good. Such a good poor person! So thoughtful the way you are sure to pay your rent on the first of every month (I noticed!) in order to stay in my good graces because, as I am sure you have learned the hard way, money isn't even always enough. You must ingratiate, supplicate, and account for my emotions and irrationality that may one day decide for any reason I deem necessary (because that is my private property right), to uproot your life and not renew your lease. Or just move on to somebody else, perhaps a family member or a friend, kick you out! I could do that! With near zero consequences!"

"..."

"Forget that my speech has gone on as long as that of a Karamazov (*shockingly this is only the first time my landlord has repeated themselves*), forget that and take this money — all of your rent — right this instant! And then drive, drive, drive off, Poor Person, and use it to cover first, last, and security at your next place because I can only imagine how outlandishly expensive that is to a tenant who's asked to float over half their net worth to secure a place in which they haven't even spent a night. And how unlikely it is for your new landlord not to begin to feel that the deposit you have given them is their money simply because they have illegally mixed it all in with their other money so that when they return to said property and discover that you have indeed lived in it at some point during your rental period that they will not hold it hostage and play chicken with you and small claims court, which you are too busy being homeless even to attend."

"..."

"Poor Person, I hope, too, that your next landlord doesn't use their mortgage payment to set the base for their rent because properties are investments right and you aren't getting any of the equity from that investment, not one lick so it isn't really fair now isn't it? So take this money, Poor Person, take it! Take it and run off with your little poor per-

son feet and this little poor person car (you have
a car, look at you go!). Go, Poor Person, GO! Get
out of here! Hide, never come back or I will do it
all to you again but worse! Because now I will be
ashamed that you didn't learn your lesson! Get out
of here, scram! Get!"

*And then my landlord releases my elbow where
beneath the pad of their thumb and upon my skin
drops of perspiration have appeared. For a moment
their skin sticks to mine, but the moisture resists the
stick, allows a separation, a parting. And then, in the
absence of touch, like when Socrates rubbed the place
where to his limbs links had been cuffed, noting how
curious it is that pleasure arises from the cessation of
pain and then back again, I experience a shiver ra-
diating from the place where they have placed a nib
of their skin upon a fragile pointed place of mine. It
has been a century since I experienced this feeling, a
century since somebody for whom I felt fondly would
softly grab the bend in my arm and ask of me the
simplest of favors, ask me to borrow a pen or pencil
or to lend them a quarter so they could buy a cinna-
mon twist from the school cafeteria. And I did it. I
did it every time because in that moment I buzzed
back like a flower buzzes back when a bee has left its
petal skin without administering the slightest sting.
An exchange of lifestuff has occurred and now, in the
aftermath, I bend and crane my face toward the sun,
begging not to be burned but basked — nurtured,
stimulated — flowed into by its awesome rays of
light. My landlord has fulfilled my dream and given
me a gift that permits me, in an instant, to forgive
their grift.*

What I Have Poured Into *Poet Meat*

I poured everything
into *Poet Meat* just as
the young man in *Andrei Rublev*
poured everything into
the founding of his bell.

Indeed, I took the extra step
of pouring molten lead
into the mouth of the
Doubting Thomas
pacing nightly about
the belfry in my head.

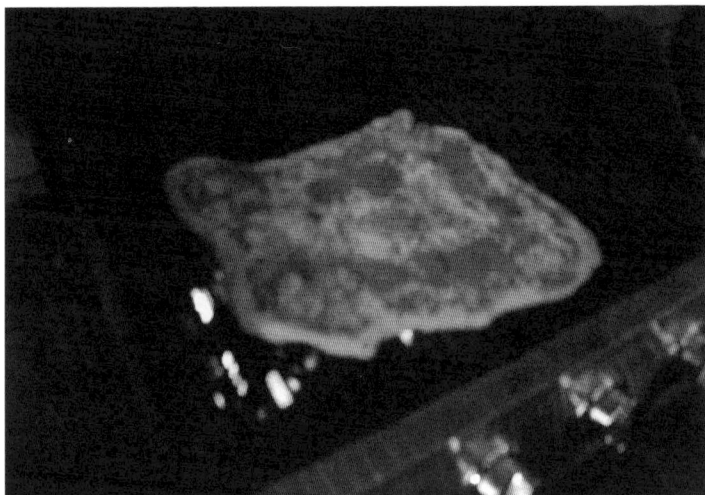

I must use this space to acknowledge the support offered by Jenny Mai Nguyen in my efforts to complete this book. In the final year of production, Jenny gave many hours towards editing and discussing the poems. She also provided constant encouragement. It's difficult to imagine how I might have completed this work without Jenny's help.

Danke, Jenny. Truly.